Joseph Haydn

Concerto for Trumpet and Orchestra
in E♭ major / Es-Dur
Hob. VIIe:1

Concerto for Cello and Orchestra
in D major / D-Dur
Hob. VIIb:2

Edited by / Herausgegeben von
Hans Ferdinand Redlich / Hans-Hubert Schönzeler

EULENBURG

EAS 167
ISBN 978-3-7957-6567-5
ISMN 979-0-2002-2557-0

© 2010 Ernst Eulenburg & Co GmbH, Mainz
for Europe excluding the British Isles
Ernst Eulenburg Ltd, London
for all other countries
Edition based on Eulenburg Study Score ETP 798 and 769
CD ℗ 2002 & © 2003 and ℗ 2000 and © 2001 Naxos Rights International Ltd

Ernst Eulenburg Ltd
48 Great Marlborough Street
London W1F 7BB

Contents / Inhalt

Concerto for Trumpet and Orchestra in E♭ major, Hob. VIIe:1

Concerto for Cello and Orchestra in D-major, Hob. VIIb:2

I. Allegro moderato 37 Track 4

II. Adagio 63 Track 5

III. Allegro 68 Track 6

Preface

Concerto for Trumpet and Orchestra in E♭ major

Composed: 1796 in Vienna
First performance: see text
Original publisher: Afa-Verlag, Berlin 1931, the work was not published during Haydn's lifetime
Instrumentation: 2 Flutes, 2 Oboes, 2 Bassoons – 2 Horns, 2 Trumpets – Timpani – Trumpet solo – Strings
Duration: ca. 15 minutes

Haydn's Trumpet Concerto must have caused some considerable astonishment at its premiere; the solo instrument confronted the audience with an entirely new soundscape never previously imagined. Such a phenomenon was due partly to Haydn's composition, but also to an innovation in instrumental construction. In the 1790s the Viennese trumpeter Anton Weidinger – after more than 20 years' experiment – introduced a trumpet that because of its technology as a keyed instrument afforded completely new ways of playing. Previously it had only been possible to perform the natural tone series on the trumpet; now, thanks to Weidinger's technological improvements the complete chromatic scale was available to the player. The new E flat trumpet did, however, have one deficiency: the dullness of the sound quality. This drawback would only be remedied with the introduction of the valve trumpet in 1813. But with this further innovation, the significance of Weidinger's achievement would also be eclipsed.

Haydn, in his Trumpet Concerto, did, however, erect a lasting musical monument to Weidinger's achievements. Haydn had returned in 1796 from his extraordinarily successful second trip to England only a few months before Weidinger approached him with his new instrument and the request for a first composition to exploit its musical potential. The new technology and the compositional challenges associated with it seem to have awakened Haydn's interest. Thus he started work to create a solo concerto that would exploit to the full the musical possibilities of the keyed trumpet: cantabile elements could now determine its musical course instead of the three-note calls especially familiar in the trumpet repertory until then. In his concerto Haydn now naturally incorporates previously impossible parts of the scale in the low register of the instrument, and there seem to be no limits to the instrument's flexibility in chromatic passages.

The new technical achievements are apparent at the beginning of the *Allegro*. Following the orchestral introduction the solo trumpet (b37ff) introduces a diatonic scale passage placed very low in its register, the realization of which would previously have been unrealistic. The first movement of the concerto – in sonata form – progresses monothematically, at first with typical trumpet fanfare motifs, but followed by a contrasting cantabile passage. The development – in C minor – impresses not least because of its fast semiquaver runs culminating in a high D flat (b110) followed almost immediately by a descent to the lowest note of the movement B flat (b117), such an extreme of register being hitherto unplayable. The extended leaps in the reprise outline the available tonal space before renewed semiquaver figuration exploits the new-found technical ease afforded by the instrument. The descending chromatic course leads to the cadenza and the brief closing coda.

The second movement begins with a cantabile melody whose opening is reminiscent of the Emperor's Hymn composed only a few months before. The *Andante* is shaped as a three-part lied form, the middle section of which would have impressed its first audience especially because of its modulation to C flat major; until this time, such a key would have been completely out of range for brass players.

In the final movement Haydn effectively displays the assets of the new instrument in a favourable light, not least thanks to the successively brilliant runs each surpassing the other. However, a recollection of the original signaling function of the trumpet is not overlooked with the fanfare-like sounds of the *Allegro* allowing those origins to be recognized within the rondo-structure.

Despite its maturity the work belatedly received its premiere four years after its composition, on 28 March 1800 as part of a benefit concert by the trumpeter Weidinger. Even after its premiere the work failed to establish itself in the concerto repertory. More than a century had to pass before the work met with a sustained success and could finally join the most popular of Haydn's works.

Sandra Borzikowski
Translation: Margit McCorkle

Preface

Concerto for Cello and Orchestra in D major

Composed: 1783 in Esterhaza
First performance: unknown
Original publisher: André, Offenbach, 1806
Instrumentation: 2 Oboes – 2 Horns – Cello solo – Strings
Duration: ca. 24 minutes

'Is Haydn's cello concerto authentic?'[1] This question preoccupied musicology into the 1950s. Yet doubts concerning authenticity were evinced not only for the Cello Concerto in D major. Originally Haydn was supposed to have composed nine cello concertos altogether. In the end only two of these works could withstand an authenticity test. The two works composed ca. 20 years apart are probably music for the court at Esterháza. In Prince Nicholas I Haydn had found an employer who – in the context of his lavish holding of court – not only promoted the music at court, but was himself also a passionate baryton player. The innumerable baryton trios commissioned by the prince, together with Haydn's baryton concertos, some of them now lost, are witness to this passion.

Haydn presumably wrote his first verifiable cello concerto, in C major, between 1762 and 1765, though its existence remained doubtful until 1961, for up to then merely a theme incipit in Haydn's autograph 'Sketch' catalogue supplied a clue to this composition. Only with the discovery of the parts in that year could the doubts be put to rest. Similarly problematical was the source situation regarding the Cello Concerto in D major originating in 1783. For a long time only the first edition from Johann André was available; following it were editions coloured by Romantic influences that sometimes distorted the composer's intention considerably. With the discovery of the autograph score in 1953 this concerto could finally be verified as an authentic Haydn composition. Besides Haydn, Anton Kraft was also considered up to this time a potential author of the Cello Concerto in D major. He had been employed from 1778 as the first cellist in the orchestra of Prince Eszterházy. Later responsibilities in the service of Count Lobkowitz took him to Vienna where he was regarded as unsurpassed on his instrument. Even if in the meantime his authorship has been conclusively ruled out, it may be taken from this that at least some of Kraft's virtuosity is reflected in Haydn's composition. The extraordinarily high technical demands presuppose at least a master on the instrument. Double stops, playing in octaves and a thorough exploitation of the higher registers are characteristic of Haydn's solo concerto, just as are the lyrical elements marking virtually the entire composition.

---

[1] Volkmann, Hans: 'Ist Haydns Cellokonzert echt?', in: *Die Musik* XXIV (1932), 427–430.

In the first movement the cantabile dominates in such a way that it even intervenes to a certain extent in the formal structure. The borders between the two themes normally structured in opposition appear in the *Allegro moderato* to be – if not abolished – then at least blurred, though. Despite the independent melodic materials, the similarities are evident as regards the layout of solo instrument and orchestra. After the orchestra first introduces the two themes (bb. 1–6), the first theme is now heard in the solo cello (b. 29). This, however, does not come unrestrictedly to the fore as the leading part. Here, the melody is also taken up again by the first violins played, however, a third lower. The violin likewise supports the soloist at the entry of the second theme (b. 50), this time, though, a sixth above the cello. In these passages at least the movement is more governed by the principle of integration than by soloistic prominence. Nonetheless, with extended virtuosic runs the soloist is given ever more space to stand out from the rather reduced orchestra sound.

The second and third movements of the concerto show analogous structures. The *Adagio* together with the closing *Allegro* with their rondo form encourage an interplay between concertante passages and those standing in a more equalized relationship of orchestra and soloist. Cello and first violin together introduce the rondo theme each time: the episodes, on the other hand, are entirely determined by the playing of the solo instrument. The contrast becomes especially evident and significant, however, in the lively final movement. In addition, this movement captivates by an effective middle section evading the minor, at whose end the soloist can once more give evidence of his competence with the most demanding octave passages.

Sandra Borzikowski
Translation: Margit McCorkle

Vorwort

Konzert für Trompete und Orchester in Es-Dur

komponiert: 1796 in Wien
Uraufführung: unbekannt
Originalverlag: Afa-Verlag, Berlin, 1931, zu Lebzeiten des Komponisten
nicht gedruckt
Orchesterbesetzung: 2 Flöten, 2 Oboen, 2 Fagotte – 2 Hörner,
2 Trompeten – Pauken – Solo-Trompete – Streicher
Spieldauer: etwa 15 Minuten

Haydns Trompetenkonzert muss bei der Uraufführung absolutes Erstaunen verursacht haben, war das Publikum doch gerade mit gänzlich neuen, noch nie gehörten Klangmöglichkeiten des Soloinstruments konfrontiert worden. Die Einzigartigkeit des Ereignisses war zum einen Haydns Komposition zu verdanken, zum anderen aber auch einer Innovation auf dem Gebiet des Instrumentenbaus. In den 1790er Jahren hatte der Wiener Hoftrompeter Anton Weidinger – nach mehr als 20 Jahren andauernden Bemühungen – schließlich eine Trompete vorgestellt, die auf Grund ihrer Klappentechnik vollkommen neue Spielweisen erlaubte. War es den alten Instrumenten bisher lediglich möglich die Naturtonreihe wiederzugeben, so konnte sich der Musiker bei seinem Spiel nun fast ausnahmslos der gesamten chromatischen Skala bedienen und erstmals annähernd unbegrenzt jegliche melodische Vorgabe realisieren. Ein Defizit hatte die neue Trompete in Es jedoch: Die neue Klappentechnik ließ sich zunächst nur zu Lasten der Klangqualität umsetzen. Erst die Einführung der Ventiltrompete im Jahr 1813 sollte diesen letzten Makel noch aus dem Weg räumen. Doch damit verblasste auch die Bedeutung von Weidingers Erfindung.

Ein bleibendes musikalisches Denkmal setzte jedoch Jospeh Haydn diesem Instrument, für das er eigens sein Trompetenkonzert in Es-Dur komponierte. Haydn war erst einige Monate zuvor von seiner außerordentlich erfolgreichen zweiten Englandreise aus London zurückgekehrt, als Weidinger im Jahr 1796 mit seinem neuen Instrument und der Bitte um eine erste Komposition für dieses an ihn herangetreten war. Die neue Technik und die damit verbundenen kompositorischen Herausforderungen scheinen das Interesse Haydns geweckt zu haben. So begab er sich ans Werk, um ein Solokonzert zu schaffen, das alle Möglichkeiten der Klappentrompete ausschöpft: Kantable Elemente anstelle der bis dahin besonders geläufigen Dreiklangsmelodik bestimmen nun den musikalischen Verlauf. Zuvor unmögliche Tonleiterausschnitte in den tiefen Lagen des Instruments baut Haydn nun ganz selbstverständlich in seine Komposition ein, und auch der Flexibilät bei chromatischen Läufen scheinen keine Grenzen gesetzt zu sein.

X

Schon zu Beginn des Allegro zeigen sich die neuen technischen Errungenschaften. Nach der orchestralen Einleitung wartet die Trompete mit einem für ihre Verhältnisse recht tief angelegten diatonischen Skalenausschnitt (T. 37ff.) auf, dessen Realisation bis zu diesem Zeitpunkt jenseits des Vorstellbaren lag. Monothematisch – zunächst mit den für die Trompete so typischen Fanfarenklängen, die aber bereits unmittelbar darauf mit einer kantablen Passage in Kontrast treten – schreitet der als Sonatenform konzipierte erste Satz des Konzerts voran. Die in c-Moll gehaltene Durchführung beeindruckt nicht zuletzt mit ihren raschen Sechzehntelläufen, die in dem vorläufigen Spitzenton des''' (T. 110) gipfeln, um gleich darauf abermals den noch kurze Zeit zuvor unspielbaren Ton b, den tiefsten Ton des Satzes anzusteuern (T. 117). Auch in der Reprise demonstrieren ausladende Sprünge den verfügbaren Tonraum bevor erneute Sechzehntelbewegungen mit scheinbarer Leichtigkeit ausgekostet werden. Der abwärts geführte chromatische Gang leitet im Anschluss zur Kadenz und der abschließenden knappen Coda über.

Der zweite Satz wird von einer kantablen Melodie eröffnet, deren erste Töne eine Art Reminiszenz an die nur wenige Monate zuvor komponierte Kaiserhymne darzustellen scheint. Das Andante wurde von Haydn als dreiteilige Liedform gestaltet, deren Mittelteil auf Grund seiner Modulation nach Ces-Dur wohl besonders beeindruckte, schien diese Tonart bis zu diesem Zeitpunkt für die Blechbläser doch noch völlig außer Reichweite.

Effektvoll rückt Haydn auch im finalen dritten Satz die Vorzüge des neuen Instruments ins rechte Licht, nicht zuletzt die brillanten Läufe scheinen mitunter das bereits Gehörte noch zu übertreffen. Doch auch eine Rückbesinnung auf die ursprüngliche Signalfunktion der Trompete ist nicht zu übersehen. Die fanfarenartigen Klänge des in Form eines Rondos gehaltenen Allegros lassen diese Wurzeln erkennen.

Trotz seiner Ausgereiftheit sollte das Werk erst vier Jahre nach seiner Komposition, am 28. März 1800, im Rahmen eines Benefizkonzertes des Trompeters Weidinger zum ersten Mal in der Öffentlichkeit erklingen. Und auch nach seiner Uraufführung konnte sich das Werk nicht etablieren. Weit mehr als 100 Jahre mussten vergehen bis es einen nachhaltigen Erfolg erzielen und sich schließlich in die beliebtesten Kompositionen Haydns einreihen konnte.

Sandra Borzikowski

Vorwort

Konzert für Violoncello und Orchester in D-Dur

komponiert: 1783 in Esterhaza
Uraufführung: unbekannt
Originalverlag: André, Offenbach, 1806
Orchesterbesetzung: 2 Oboen – 2 Hörner – Solo-Cello – Streicher
Spieldauer: etwa 24 Minuten

„Ist Haydns Cellokonzert echt?"[1] Diese Frage beschäftigte die Musikwissenschaft bis in die 1950er Jahre hinein. Doch nicht nur dem Cellokonzert in D-Dur wurden Zweifel bezüglich seiner Authentizität entgegengebracht. Insgesamt neun Cellokonzerte soll Haydn ursprünglich geschaffen haben. Letztendlich konnten nur zwei dieser Werke einer Authentizitätsprüfung standhalten. Bei den beiden im Abstand von ca. 20 Jahren komponierten Werken handelt es sich wohl um Musik für den Hof von Esterháza. In Fürst Nikolaus I. hatte Haydn einen Dienstherrn gefunden, der die Musik am Hofe nicht nur – im Rahmen seiner aufwändigen Hofhaltung – förderte, sondern selbst leidenschaftlicher Baryton-Spieler war. Die unzähligen vom Fürsten in Auftrag gegebenen Baryton-Trios sowie die heute zum Teil verschollenen Baryton-Konzerte Haydns zeugen von dieser Passion.

Sein erstes nachweisbares Cellokonzert in C-Dur schrieb Haydn vermutlich zwischen 1762 und 1765. Dessen Existenz blieb allerdings bis zum Jahr 1961 fragwürdig, da bis dahin lediglich ein Themenincipit in Haydns eigenhändigem „Entwurf"-Katalog einen Anhaltspunkt für diese Komposition lieferte. Erst die in jenem Jahr aufgefundene Stimmenabschrift konnte die Zweifel beseitigen. Ähnlich problematisch stellte sich die Quellenlage in Bezug auf das 1783 entstandene Cellokonzert in D-Dur dar. Lange Zeit lag nur der Erstdruck von Johann André vor, dem von romantischen Einflüssen gefärbte Ausgaben folgten, die zum Teil die Intention des Komponisten erheblich verfälschten. Mit der Entdeckung des Autographs im Jahre 1953 konnte dieses Konzert schließlich als authentische Komposition Haydns verifiziert werden. Bis zu diesem Zeitpunkt wurde neben Haydn auch Anton Kraft als potentieller Autor des Cellokonzertes in D-Dur in Betracht gezogen. Dieser war seit 1778 als erster Cellist in der Kapelle des Fürsten Eszterházy angestellt. Spätere Verpflichtungen führten ihn nach Wien in die Dienste des Grafen Lobkowitz, wo er als unübertroffen auf seinem Instrument galt. Auch wenn seine Urheberschaft mittlerweile zweifelsfrei ausgeschlossen worden ist, darf man wohl davon ausgehen, dass sich zumindest ein Teil von Krafts Virtuosentum in Haydns Komposition spiegelt. Die außerordentlich hohen spieltechnischen Anforderungen setzen

---

[1] Volkmann, Hans: „Ist Haydns Cellokonzert echt?", in: *Die Musik* XXIV (1932), S. 427–430.

zumindest einen Meister am Instrument voraus. Doppelgriffe, Oktavspiel und das Ausreizen der hohen Lagen sind charakteristisch für Haydns Solokonzert, ebenso wie die lyrischen Elemente die nahezu die gesamte Komposition prägen.

Im ersten Satz dominiert die Kantabilität derart, dass sie sogar in gewissem Maße in die formale Gestaltung eingreift. Die Grenze zwischen den beiden üblicherweise konträr angelegten Themen scheint im Allegro moderato – wenn nicht aufgehoben – dann doch zumindest verwischt zu sein. Trotz des eigenständigen melodischen Materials sind die Ähnlichkeiten in Bezug auf Disposition von Soloinstrument und Orchester evident. Nach einer erstmaligen Vorstellung beider Themen durch das Orchester (T. 1–6) erklingt das erste Thema nun im Solocello (T. 29). Doch dieses tritt nicht als uneingeschränkt führende Stimme hervor. Die Melodie wird auch hier wieder von der ersten Violine aufgegriffen, die sie jedoch eine Terz tiefer intoniert. Ebenso unterstützt sie den Solisten beim Einsatz des zweiten Themas (T. 50), dieses Mal allerdings eine Sexte über dem Cello. Zumindest an diesen Stellen ist der Satz mehr vom Prinzip der Integration als von solistischem Exponieren beherrscht. Dennoch wird dem Solist immer wieder Raum gegeben, sich mit ausgedehnten, virtuos geführten Läufen vom eher reduzierten Orchesterklang abzuheben.

Analoge Strukturen weisen auch der zweite sowie der dritte Satz des Konzertes auf. Sowohl das Adagio als auch das abschließende Allegro begünstigen mit ihrer Rondoform ein Wechselspiel zwischen konzertanten und den eher in einem ausgeglichenen Verhältnis von Orchester und Solist stehenden Passagen. Cello und erste Geige stellen jeweils gemeinsam das Rondothema vor, die Zwischenteile hingegen werden ganz vom Spiel des Soloinstruments bestimmt. Besonders signifikant tritt der Kontrast jedoch im ausgelassenen Finalsatz hervor. Dieser besticht zudem durch einen effektvollen nach Moll ausweichenden Mittelteil, zu dessen Ende hin der Solist nochmals seine Fähigkeiten anhand der äußerst anspruchsvollen Oktavgänge unter Beweis stellen kann.

Sandra Borzikowski

Trumpet Concerto

Joseph Haydn
(1732–1809)

Edited by Hans Ferdinand Redlich
© 2010 Ernst Eulenburg Ltd, London
and Ernst Eulenburg & Co GmbH, Mainz

4

6

7

EAS 167

8

9

10

12

130

EAS 167

14

16

II.

18

20

III.

22

24

EAS 167

28

30

EAS 167

32

33

34

Cello Concerto

Joseph Haydn
(1732–1809)

I

Allegro moderato

EAS 167

Edited by Hans-Hubert Schönzeler
© 2010 Ernst Eulenburg Ltd, London
and Ernst Eulenburg & Co GmbH, Mainz

38

44

50

70

Vc.-S.

Vl.

Vla.

Vc.
e Cb.

Cor.
(D)

Vc.-S.

Vl.

Vla.

Vc.
e Cb.

Ob.

Cor.
(D)

Vc.-S.

Vl.

Vla.

Vc.
e Cb.

48

49

50

51

53

EAS 167

54

55

EAS 167

56

EAS 167

59

EAS 167

Flautino

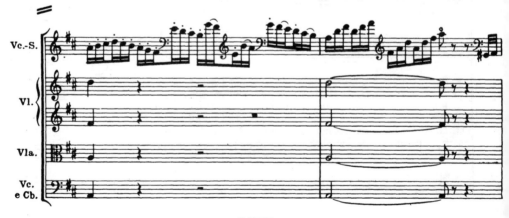

62

II

66

68

III

Allegro

71

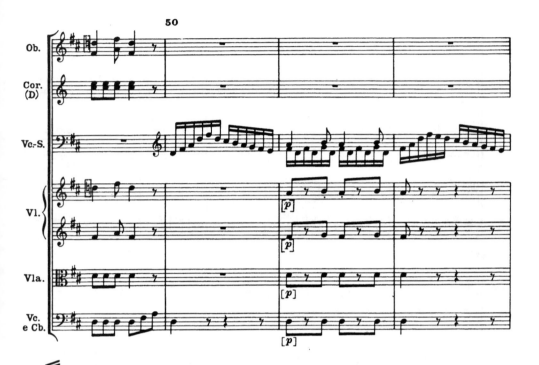

EAS 167

72

80

Fine

Laus deo.

Printed in China